And Yet

on becoming a wounded worshipper

---

by Abbie Lynn Abbott

ISBN: 978-1-7375914-0-5

And Yet - on becoming a wounded worshipper by Abbie Lynn Abbott

Editor: Sarah Land

Designed by: Heather Dauphiny

Consultant Editor: Emily Osburne

Contents

A note from the author...

Thank you for picking up my book. Thank you for at least considering reading the words I've written. Thank you for giving space for my story.

I'll be honest. Writing this book has been one of the most vulnerable things I have ever done. I have put myself on these pages. My thoughts. My emotions. My journey. Me.

Although writing *And Yet* has been a vulnerable process for me, I know that reading it might be just as vulnerable for you. I don't know where you are as you open the pages of this book. Maybe you have recently suffered great loss and are in the crushing depths of sorrow. I pray there is comfort to be found here.

Maybe you are a bit farther down the road of your grief journey and are wrestling with the unwelcome familiarity of your new normal. I pray there is peace to be found here.

Maybe you have yet to walk through sorrow, mourning, or pain and are fearful of the day on which trauma may come your way. I pray there is hope to be found here.

And maybe you are simply an avid reader and are reading out of curiosity. I pray there is life to be found here.

If you are reading *And Yet* in hopes of taking your own steps toward healing, I encourage you to consider using the journal prompts provided at the end of the book. Each chapter has its own prompt. Maybe dust off the cover of that journal you received as a gift on your last birthday and simply write what you are thinking and feeling. Allow God to bring healing to your own heart as you read what He has done in mine.

Remember - this may not be a "happy ending" kind of book, but it is a beautiful story.

Thank you, again, for taking the time to read my book. I am honored to share my story with you. Maybe someday you can share yours with me.

Wounded and Worshipping...

Abbie

To my Sweet Momma – the first person to ever tell me I should write a book. Oh, how I wish you were here to read it. Thank you for always being my fan. I miss you more than words can say. Love you – infinity...

1 Even Now

As I step out of the car, the heel of my boot clicks louder than it should. I stop in my tracks and quickly look down. Not knowing what it is I am expecting, I hold my breath. Yet nothing extraordinary has happened. Nothing is out of the ordinary or significant about the sound of the heels on the hard ground. Except that they aren't actually my heels. They are her heels. The cute two-inch heeled boots that I talked her into buying because they just "looked like her." The stylish ankle boots that I always asked to borrow whenever I was in town. The fashionable, yet sensible, heels that she wore with class and confidence. They were her heels. Now they are my heels. And I don't want them. I don't want this. I don't want to be here - hearing these sounds, smelling these smells, feeling these feelings, doing these things. I don't want anything to do with this.

But I don't get a choice. Not in this.

But you do, God. You have a choice. Even now... flowers delivered, visitation over... Even now you have a choice, Lord. You could still heal her. You could still bring her back to life. You could do it... Will you please?

Taking a step toward the door, my borrowed brown leather heeled boots hitting the cold, black pavement, everything seems to be moving in slow motion. And yet, at the same time, it seems as though everything is moving far too fast for me to keep up. I wonder if I might find myself somehow missing this extremely important (mind you - extremely unwelcome and fully hated) day. I decide to use the remaining minutes with intentionality. I choose to be present. Mindful. Aware.

I take a few more steps toward the door and I catch my brother's eye. My baby brother. He's a full 9 inches taller than me, larger than life, vibrant - and his tears are freely flowing down his face. Five of his closest friends stand with him. The beautifully carved wooden box sits in between them. 1, 2, 3, lift. The weight of the entire world resting on my brother's shoulders. On all of our shoulders. I watch him intensely as the quiet processional carries the casket indoors. I can see it in his eyes. Our thoughts are identical. "I don't want this. I don't want to be here - hearing these sounds, smelling these smells, feeling these feelings, doing these things. I don't want anything to do with this."

But we don't get a choice. Not in this.

But you do, God. You have a choice. Even now... funeral completed, casket closed... Even now you have a choice, Lord. You could still heal her. You could still bring her back to life. You could do it... Will you please?

As I am about to step through the door, my precious husband's ever supportive hand on my back, I feel my sister grasp my fingers. My big sister. She's the leader, brilliantly articulate, fashionable - and her hands are desperate for something on which to hold. Her husband and children walking alongside her, just as mine walk alongside me. I gaze at her profile as she stares down the task before us. I can see it in her shoulders. She, my rock solid sister, is thinking the exact same thoughts. "I don't want this. I don't want to be here - hearing these sounds, smellings these smells, feeling these feelings, doing these things. I don't want anything to do with this."

But we don't get a choice. Not in this.

But you do, God. You have a choice. Even now... tears wept, prayers uttered... Even now you have a choice, Lord. You could still heal her. You could still bring her back to life. You could do it... Will you please?

We step through the doors. The mausoleum is surprisingly welcoming. Uncomfortably inviting. Eerily calm. We walk past the friends and family who have already made it to the cemetery, and it is clear that everyone is feeling the weight of this unwelcome moment. As I force myself to scan the room - committing to memory what I can, attempting to remember the moments that I begged would not come to fruition, searching for a glimmer of hope in the midst of this darkest of moments - I have a realization. We are all the same. Not one of us wants this. Not me. Not my brother or my sister. Not my dad, my children, my nieces, my husband. Not her brothers. Not her best friends. Not one of us wants to be here - hearing these sounds, smellings these smells, feelings these feelings, doing these things. Not one of us wants anything to do with this.

But again, we don't get a choice. Not in this.

But you do, God. You have a choice. Even now... worlds shattered, hopes dashed, dreams undone... Even now you have a choice, Lord. You could still heal her. You could still bring her back to life. You could do it... Will you please?

My compassionate and empathetic husband (our pastor, in the truest sense of the word), says a few more words to close out the time. We pray. The casket is placed within her pre-reserved spot in the wall of the mausoleum. Our task is finished, and I feel the ground give way. Her cute little heeled boots are unable to do their job. They can no longer keep my knees from buckling underneath me. I can't stand any longer and my breath becomes difficult to catch. My heart simultaneously beats out of my chest and seems to simply stop mid-beat. How could this be? It is finished. And I don't want this. I don't want to be here - hearing these sounds, smelling these smells, feeling these feelings, doing these things. I am tempted to scream at the top of my lungs. I don't want anything to do with this.

But I don't get a choice. Not in this.

But you did, God. You did have a choice. You could have healed her. You could have brought her back to life. You could have done it.

You didn't.

Why not?

What now?

2 *Wounded*

wounded (adj.) – inflicted with an injury

synonyms include: crushed, battered, marred, bruised, damaged, beaten

Wounded. No other word seems to more clearly describe me as I leave the cemetery on the day of my mother's funeral. Sweet Momma. My best friend. My protector. My confidant. My biggest fan. My momma bear, in every sense of the word. And now? Now she is gone. I have lost a piece of me. An ever present, always encouraging, fully understanding, unbelievably organized, sometimes nagging, forever loving piece of me. And I have absolutely no idea how to move forward.

I am wounded.

No one can ever fully understand what it will mean

for our family to relearn how to function without her presence in our lives. To be honest though, the void of Sweet Momma is only part of the wounding. Truth be told, the deeper part of the wounding is in the shattered hope of what could have been. The crushed, battered, marred, bruised, damaged, and beaten trust in what we not only hoped, but truly believed, God was going to do.

Have you ever prayed so desperately for something, knowing with full certainty that the something for which you are praying is good and right for the world?

But He doesn't make it happen...

Have you ever begged God to show up in a very real and tangible way, having not an ounce of doubt as to His willingness or faithfulness to do so?

But He doesn't come through...

Have you ever been so consumed by your own hopes and dreams, your own understanding of reality, that you are wholly unable to see even the slightest possibility that God might have another plan?

And He doesn't meet your expectations...

Have you ever worshipped God in advance for the thing you have full confidence He is going to do?

And He simply doesn't do it...

But you did, God. You did have a choice. You could have

*healed her. You could have brought her back to life. You could
have done it. You didn't. Why not? What now?*

From the day we learned of Momma's cancer diagnosis,
to just seven short months later, I prayed. I begged. I
worshipped God, with unwavering confidence that He
was going to make it happen. That He was going to
come through for us. That He would not just meet, but
maybe even exceed our expectations. I worshipped Him
in advance for the healing He was going to bring to
Sweet Momma's body. He was going to beat cancer for
her. For us. For me.

But He didn't.

Sweet Momma took her final breaths at 12:01pm on
Tuesday, October 23, 2018. And that day - although
utterly devastating, completely earth shattering, and
mind numbingly traumatic - was not the day on which
I realized the depth of my woundedness. I didn't truly
recognize my status as being a wounded soul... Not
yet. Not fully... Not until the moment I finally came to
grips with the fact that God was not going to heal my
Momma.

You see, I truly believe God has the power to heal. I
know without a shadow of a doubt that He could have
healed her. And my friends, I really and truly did believe
that He could (and would) heal her, even up until the
wall in the mausoleum was closed.

Those prayers were real. I meant every single word.

But you do, God. You have a choice. Even now... flowers delivered, visitation over... funeral completed, casket closed... tears wept, prayers uttered... worlds shattered, hopes dashed, dreams undone... Even now you have a choice, Lord. You could still heal her. You could still bring her back to life. You could do it... Will you please?

As I stood in the cemetery, on that dreary October afternoon, I was shocked. I was absolutely devastated. Injured, crushed, battered, marred, bruised, damaged, and beaten.

Wounded.

As I fell to my knees, losing my grip on reality for a moment, confused by what had just happened... or not happened rather... I meant that prayer too.

But you did, God. You did have a choice. You could have healed her. You could have brought her back to life. You could have done it. You didn't. Why not? What now?

Why not?

Why didn't He heal her?

And what now, now that grief has entered my world?

The world moves on. Life keeps happening all around me. And grief takes over every single particle of my being. Terrifying, disgusting, angry, lonely grief.

A new question begins creeping into my thoughts.

How do I worship you now?

I'm not really asking the question though. I'm not really asking, because I'm not really listening. I'm not really listening, because I don't want to know the answer. I don't want to know the answer, because now I am the one who has a choice. I didn't have a choice in her healing, but I do have a choice in this. I'm not really asking... because I don't have to.

I am defiant in my woundedness.

I eat a pint of ice cream for lunch.

I binge watch old tv shows.

I cancel doctor appointments.

I drink more wine than I should and less water than I need.

Because I can.

I hide in a clothing rack at Target (like literally, the "crouching underneath the clothes so as not to be seen" type of hiding) so that I don't have to talk to anyone.

I lie to my friends about why I need their help picking

up my kids from school, simply so I don't have to get dressed and leave the house.

I sign up for a grocery delivery service so that I can have a stranger bring our food rather than risk running into someone I know.

Because I don't have to.

I run more miles than my weary body can handle.

I take hour long showers multiple times a day.

I sleep all day long.

Because I can.

And then I don't exercise.

I don't shower.

I don't sleep.

Because I don't have to.

I leave emails and text messages unread, phone calls unanswered.

I take walks with absolutely no destination in mind. Just

walk… as long as I want.

I read every book I can get my hands on, except my Bible.

I cry.

I scream.

I sit in silence.

Because I can.

I don't write.

I don't dance.

I don't sing.

And I certainly don't ask.

Because I don't have to.

How do I worship you now?

I don't want to know.

Wounded. No other word seems to more clearly describe me as I grieve. And I have absolutely no idea how to move forward.

3 Not Alone

For the first few weeks after Momma's funeral, I don't go to church. I just can't. Part of me doesn't want to go, and part of me doesn't know how. As I build up my wall of grief, I am scared God will break through. And I am simply not ready for him to show up. So, for weeks, I just don't go.

Not going to church is a big deal for me. You see - church has always been a safe place for me. Always. I know that is not the case for a lot of people, and if that is you - I am so sorry. I believe the church should be safe for all of us, no matter where we are on our journey. For me, church has been a safe place to exist. A place to gain perspective, gather healing, and grow in hope. Is church still a safe place for me? Maybe. Is it possible I need to exist in that safe space again - to gain perspective, gather healing, and grow in hope? Likely.

Yet, my defiant grief runs deep. I don't go. I choose not to go.

Because I don't have to.

Now, weeks later, I am back at church. Sitting in the back row, as far away from the stage as possible, in the shadows. Arriving late. Leaving early. My muscles are tense, as if I am in a serious fight or flight situation, and I have no idea which to choose.

I am hoping for anonymity. Willing the shadows to hide me. Lurking in the darkness. Avoiding any glimmer of light. Everything in my body is telling me to run, but I am frozen to the cushioned seat in the very back of the old movie theater turned sanctuary, unable to even stand... let alone run. Fight, it is.

The entire service, every single moment, is shaped around God's goodness.

God's goodness? I just can't. I literally cannot.

Where is your goodness now, God?

The band is made up of beautiful souls whom I consider to be friends, but in my grief-laden haze they look like complete strangers. The music sounds hauntingly familiar, but the words no longer make sense. The air is filled with the sweet voices of those standing around me, yet I want nothing more than to cover my ears and yell over the noise.

You're a good, good Father? You're never gonna let me down? Your kindness leads me? I just can't. I literally cannot.

Where is your goodness now, God?

I barely even listen to the words spoken during the sermon. Every second that I remain in that room, the more betrayed I feel. Church has always been my place of solace. Worship has always been my source of comfort. God has always been my refuge. Digging my heels into defiant grief, anger begins to take hold. I just can't. I literally cannot.

Where is your goodness now, God?

Fists held tightly in my lap, jaw clenched, tears streaming steadily down my cheeks - I find myself asking the one question I do not want to ask.

How do I worship you now?

I am weeping now. I look down, trying (and failing) to catch my breath. The room that had just seconds earlier been a complete blur, now comes into full focus. I see her brown leather boots. The cute two-inch heeled boots that I wore to the cemetery. The same boots that failed to keep my knees from buckling underneath me on that dreadful day. They still feel borrowed. They were her boots. Now they are my boots. And I still don't want them. I still don't want this.

Fight, it is.

God, I don't want to be here – hearing these sounds, smelling these smells, feeling these feelings, doing these things. I don't want anything to do with this. How do I worship you now?

I feel my husband's reassuring hand on my back. I am startled at first. Intensely battling within, full on fight mode, wrestling with God - I had momentarily forgotten that I am not alone. Garry's warm and gentle hand reminds me of his presence. His kind, patient, loving, supportive, comforting presence. I am not alone.

Breathe in.

I am not alone.

Breathe out.

I am not alone.

For the first time in a very long time I feel something close to gratitude.

4 two truths

Breathe in.

I am not alone.

Breathe out.

I am not alone.

For the first time in a very long time I feel something close to gratitude.

I am not alone.

As I stand to leave the dark sanctuary, wanting to escape before the service ends and anyone might recognize my grief stricken self, two distinctly opposing thoughts spring up at the exact same moment. I feel two starkly different truths, absolutely raging against each other.

First, I feel a desperate need to remember that I am not alone. I almost frantically reach for Garry's hand. Something deep within wants to cling to the truth that I am not alone - both in this very moment, my first time back at church in weeks; and in the continuing seconds, minutes, hours, days, weeks, and months ahead. I need to know, in my very being, that I am not alone.

At the exact same time, the second thought is just as wholly prevalent. I want to be alone. No one can understand the loss I am walking. No one can grasp the void I have been handed. No one is allowed to try to empathize, because no one really knows. Whether any of those "no one" statements are true, I feel them with my whole heart. A guttural desire for isolation takes up residence in the very same being that needs to know she is not alone.

I feel alone, but I am not alone.

I feel alone, and I want to be alone.

Two very different truths, yet both unwaveringly real.

Grief is lonely and isolating. At least, my grief is lonely and isolating. I just want to be alone. When I say the words, "no one can understand," and, "no one knows," I mean those words. Every fiber of my being means those words. In my darkest moments of grief, I feel anger towards anyone who even tries to understand. How could you possibly know? She was my best friend, my confidant, my biggest fan, my unconditionally loving mother. She was mine. You can't know.

In the moments of grief that hold a bit more clarity though, I am aware of the reality that every single person who ever came into contact with Sweet Momma knows. Whether I want them to or not, everyone who knew her has at least some level of understanding. She was truly a gem, in the most beautiful sense of the word, and no one ever left her presence without knowing it.

On the day we took Sweet Momma to the emergency room, we were simply following doctor's orders. "Go have them run some tests and just double check that the fever she is experiencing is simply a side effect of her cancer treatments. I'll let them know you are on your way."

We were sure this would simply be a one-day detour to a lovely week of quality family time. We had not one tiny idea that we were in for the most traumatic and heart wrenching week and a half any of us has ever walked, ultimately ending with the loss of the most precious woman in our lives. So, as we sat in her brightly lit ER room, discussing what meals we would make over the coming days while I was in town, our hearts were fairly light.

If it weren't for the fluorescent lighting, white coats, scrubs, and beeping machines with wires attached to Momma, you would have thought we were just enjoying an afternoon in the serene sunroom at our parents' farmhouse. My baby brother and I played trivia with Momma. We ate soup and sandwiches for lunch. We drank too much coffee. We Face Timed with our Colorado residing sister. We looked up the origin of the Yiddish phrase "oy vey" – a commonly spoken phrase in our family, typically accompanied by many a roll of the eyes. We made our Daddy cry with laughter with our bad jokes and storytelling. We played cards. We made Momma laugh to the point that she almost kicked us out because her cancer ridden body was aching from the exertion. Simply put, as strange as it may seem, we had fun.

The attending emergency room doctor came into Momma's little ER space and talked with her a bit about her diagnosis, treatment, and current symptoms. He explained some of the tests they planned to run. He gave us a chance to ask questions. Then he put his hand on Momma's shoulder and smiled as he said, "Don't you know that bad things happen to the nicest people? Stop being so damn nice. Go home and kick the cat."

Every single person who ever came into contact with Sweet Momma knows, and somehow that feels both comforting and unfair.

I feel alone, but I am not alone. Everyone who knew her has at least some level of understanding. Everyone feels the void of her existence to some extent. I am not alone.

I feel alone, and I want to be alone. I feel anger towards anyone who even tries to understand. How could you possibly know? She was my best friend, my confidant, my biggest fan, my unconditionally loving mother. She was mine. You can't know.

Two very different truths, yet both unwaveringly real.

When the doctor came in to break the news that Momma would not be heading home just yet, we were bummed, but not devastated. She would spend a day or two in the hospital until her fever subsided and the tests could give more insight into what exactly was happening in her tiny little five foot nothing body. These things happen with cancer journeys. Simply a little detour before Momma could "go home and kick the cat," so to speak.

Over the course of the next few days, many an hour is spent listening to music. One afternoon, as I find myself gifted with a few minutes alone with Momma, we listen to some of our favorite worship songs. The air outside is cold and blustery. The window reveals a world that continues to move through the cloudy, fall day with hustle and bustle. Unlike us, snuggled up in warm blankets and listening to beautiful melodies and harmonies. I look over at Momma, her eyes closed, her face calm, her hand holding the handmade wooden cross, lovingly made by my brother in law. The words playing over the little cell phone speaker are haunting.

when peace like a river attendeth my way,

when sorrows like sea billows roll;

whatever my lot, thou hast taught me to say,

it is well, it is well, with my soul

it is well (it is well)

with my soul (with my soul)

it is well, it is well, with my soul.

Momma opens her piercingly blue eyes and looks at me.

"Ab, no matter what happens, don't ever forget that God is good. Don't ever forget that He is faithful. And don't ever forget that He is with you always. Everything is going to be okay."

I blink back the tears and smile at her, unaware of how often I will need to remember those words over the coming seconds, minutes, hours, days, weeks, months, and even years.

Now weeks later, sitting quietly in my husband's car, happy Christmas lights unknowingly taunting me as we drive home from church, I find myself reliving those minutes in the hospital room. I want to go back to that moment. I want to be in my Momma's kind and encouraging presence. I want to ask her to tell me more. I want her to tell me everything is going to be okay. I want to watch her listen to the music – eyes closed, face calm, cross in hand.

But alas, I am here, leaving church, wrestling with my two starkly opposing truths.

I feel alone, but I am not alone.

I feel alone, and I want to be alone.

God, I don't want to be here - hearing these sounds, smelling these smells, feeling these feelings, doing these things. I don't want anything to do with this. How do I worship you now?

Driving along in silence, the overly cheerful Christmas lights continue to mock me. Garry reaches over and gently places his hand on my knee.

Breathe in.

I am not alone.

Breathe out.

I am not alone.

That feeling that is something close to gratitude – the one I felt as I sat weeping in the cold dark sanctuary just minutes before – that feeling begins to grow.

I am not alone. Thank you, Jesus. I am not alone.

5 Words On The Page

As the days of lonely grief continue, that feeling that is something close to gratitude (the one I felt as I sat weeping in the cold, dark sanctuary: the one that began to grow as we silently drove home) – that feeling continues to take up space in my being.

I am not alone. Thank you, Jesus. I am not alone.

I feel it touching those quiet corners of pain where I find myself wanting to hide.

I am not alone. Thank you, Jesus. I am not alone.

I feel it reaching into the hardest of moments, as the darkness threatens to overtake me.

I am not alone. Thank you, Jesus. I am not alone.

A few days later, sitting in the coffee nook of our kitchen window, I am reminded of an evening just a few weeks back. An evening in August of 2018, just a little over two months before we would lose my precious mother to cancer. On that particular night I was standing in the middle of the stage in the sanctuary of our church, speaking to a precious group of women on the topic of worship, oblivious to the coming reckoning. My world had been shaken by Momma's diagnosis and I was hurt by our current reality, but I remained fully confident in God's willingness to show up for us. I was sure.

I began my time on that stage by simply defining the word worship.

Worship is the expression of reverence and adoration.

I went on to unpack what it means to worship God, to live a lifestyle of worship. How to live in such a way that our ability to worship the Lord flows, not simply out of the earthly gifts He has given us, but out of gratitude for the love, grace, and mercy He gives us each and every single day. I talked about what it means to worship God both when we can readily and easily see His goodness, and when His goodness is much less obvious. Worshipping in the good and in the bad. I talked about finding the blessings in the midst of the darkness.

And I meant every single word I spoke that night. Every single word.

But I wasn't wounded.

Not really. Not yet.

Now, sitting in the coffee nook of our kitchen window, staring blindly out at the afternoon sun, I begin to wonder. Are the words I spoke then still true now? Do I still mean every single word? Now that I am wounded, deeply and harshly wounded, would I still stand in the middle of that stage in the sanctuary of our church, speaking on the topic of worship, uttering the same convictions and encouragements?

Even though I am in deep thought over the idea of worship, the word gratitude keeps coming to mind. I pick up my phone and, mostly in an effort to prove myself wrong more than anything else, I do a quick definition search.

Worship – the expression of reverence and adoration.

Gratitude – a readiness to show appreciation or adoration for.

There it is, in black and white. Plain as day. Perfectly clear. Once I see it, I can't unsee it. I can't "prove myself wrong" on this one.

Adoration.

The one word connection between gratitude and worship is inescapable, and I begin to see the answer to the question I have been trying not to ask.

How do I worship you now?

Gratitude. Adoration. Worship.

The questions begin to flow. All of the questions I don't want to ask, because I don't want to listen. All of the questions I don't want to ask, because I am not ready for an answer. All of the questions I don't want to ask, because, quite simply – I don't have to.

I begin to ask them now.

How do I worship you now?

Where is your goodness?

Gratitude for what?

Adoration for what?

How do I worship you now?

Almost instinctively, I turn to a verse that I remember reading on the night that I spoke about worship. I don't want to read it. I know what it is going to say. But I can't stop myself.

"Every good and perfect gift is from above, coming down from the Father of the heavenly lights, who does not change like shifting shadows." James 1:17

If you are anything like me, talking about good and

perfect gifts is easy when life goes as planned. Making lists of the blessings in our daily lives comes naturally when God does what we want Him to do. But what now? When He doesn't make it happen? When He doesn't come through? When He doesn't meet our expectations? When He certainly could have done the thing, and He simply doesn't do it?

But you did, God. You did have a choice. You could have healed her. You could have brought her back to life. You could have done it. You didn't. Why not? What now?

I stare at the words on the page.

"…who does not change like shifting shadows."

Does not change? Is that true, God? It seems everything has changed. My life. The world. You. How do I worship you now?

It is as if my eyes have blurred to the entire world except the words on the page.

"…who does not change like shifting shadows."

Does not change? Is it possible that is actually true, God? It seems everything has changed. My life. The world. You. How do I worship you now?

I'm not even seeing the words on the page anymore. They are simply playing over and over in my head. Repeating, both as a statement and in question form.

"…who does not change like shifting shadows."

Does not change? I need that to be true, God. It seems everything has changed. My life. The world. You. How do I worship you now?

Still sitting in the coffee nook of our kitchen window, I shake my head and grab my now room temperature coffee. My eyes come back into focus and I look out at the afternoon sun. I spot a butterfly. A beautiful black and orange butterfly is hovering peacefully over the bright purple flowers in our side yard. Beautiful. Calm.

Breathe in.

I am not alone.

Breathe out.

I am not alone.

There it is again. That feeling. Touching the loneliness. Reaching into the darkness.

Gratitude.

I am not alone. Thank you, Jesus. I am not alone.

I am not sure how long I watch as the butterfly contentedly flutters from one flower to the next in search of the next drop of sweet nectar, but soon another joins the first. They begin to twirl in the air around each other, both effortlessly flying to and fro. It is as if they are dancing the most intricate choreography, set to a melody only they can hear. Tears are streaming down my cheeks. I feel as though I am being offered a front row seat to a grand performance that was planned solely for me. What a gift.

My breath catches in my lungs and I can't stop the overwhelming sobs from coming. What a gift. A beautiful gift. A good and perfect gift.

"Every good and perfect gift is from above, coming down from the Father of the heavenly lights, who does not change like shifting shadows."

Breathe in. Gratitude.

Thank you for the gift of this moment.

Breathe out. Adoration.

You made this, God. You did this.

I glance down and stare at the words on the page for a moment.

"...who does not change like shifting shadows."

My eyes blur to the entire world, except for the words on the page.

"...who does not change like shifting shadows."

I take a deep breath and look up, watching the butterflies again, not even seeing the words on the page anymore.

Once again, they begin to play over and over in my head.

"...who does not change like shifting shadows."

The butterflies continue their intricate choreography and I tilt my head to the side as I watch. I can't help but notice. The words playing over and over in my head have become the melody to which the butterflies are dancing. The detailed movement seems to have been created for this exact melody.

"Every good and perfect gift is from above, coming down from the Father of the heavenly lights, who does not change like shifting shadows."

Does not change. Help me to see that it is true, God. Help me to worship you now.

6 It Can Be Both

Breathe in.

I am not alone.

Breathe out.

Thank you, Jesus.

Breathe in. Gratitude.

Thank you for the gift of this moment.

Breathe out. Adoration.

You made this, God. You did this.

Gratitude. Adoration. Worship.

I am attempting to incorporate the three into my every day.

The gratitude and adoration moments begin to come more easily, but the worship step... Worship is still pretty clunky. Unnatural. Uneasy and unsure. The questions keep coming, even as I force myself to find moments for which to express gratitude.

How do I worship you now?

Why not?

What now?

Where is your goodness?

How do I worship you now?

Part of me wants nothing to do with moving forward and finding healing. Part of me wants to just cling to the hurt, anger, and disappointment. Sit in the muck and mire. Stay wounded.

But a larger part of me starts to recognize my need for more. Part of me knows I have to take steps – even small, seemingly insignificant steps. Small steps toward healing.

So, I take the steps. I put myself in the right places – go to church, read my Bible, listen to worship music, stop isolating. I attempt to say the right things – quote scripture, pray, speak life, be honest. I place one vulnerable foot in front of the other, hoping that eventually my wounded heart will heal. Small steps toward healing.

Sometimes it feels like two steps forward, one step back. One step forward, two steps back. But I take the steps. I do the things. Stop isolating. Be honest. One vulnerable foot in front of the other. Small steps toward healing.

Gratitude. Adoration. Worship.

I am attempting to incorporate the three into my every day.

Breathe in.

I am not alone.

Breathe out.

Thank you, Jesus.

Breathe in. Gratitude.

Thank you for the gift of this moment.

Breathe out. Adoration.

You made this, God. You did this.

I am relearning how to worship. I am practicing. I am beginning to remember what it means to find God's blessings, even in the midst of the hard. I am becoming a wounded worshipper.

Sometimes the things for which I express gratitude and adoration are as simple as the fact that I woke up in the morning, or I have a roof over my head. Other times

I find myself seeing the larger, more extravagant gifts and graces – my three children, my loving husband, the delicious cup of coffee in my hands, the cute clothes in my closet, the cars in our driveway, the laughter a funny story brings, the memories that bring me to my knees in pain, our community, my inner circle. I find myself less ashamed to find the good in the midst of the pain. I begin to realize that it can be both. Life can be both painful and beautiful. Life can be both good and hard. It can be both.

For so many seconds, minutes, hours, days, weeks, and even months after losing Sweet Momma, the wound was all I could see. I couldn't hear, taste, touch, or smell anything other than the wound.

Wounded was all I could be.

Now, as the seconds, minutes, hours, days, weeks, and months march on, wounded continues to be part of my identity – but wounded is not my only identity. The wound no longer consumes every fiber of my senses. I begin to be able to see, hear, taste, touch, and smell the world around me again. I smile. I laugh. I dance, sing, cry, live.

Wounded is part of me, but wounded is not all of me. It can be both.

I am reminded of the words in Isaiah 61:3. "...He provides for those who grieve – He bestows on them a crown of beauty instead of ashes; the oil of joy instead of mourning, and a garment of praise instead of a spirit of despair."

I actually feel as though I am wearing a crown of beauty. I am taking the steps. I am doing the things. Stop isolating. Be honest. One vulnerable foot in front of the other. Small steps toward healing.

Breathe in.

I am not alone.

Breathe out.

Thank you, Jesus.

Breathe in. Gratitude.

Thank you for the gift of this moment.

Breathe out. Adoration.

You made this, God. You did this.

One morning, after getting my kids off to school and my husband off to work, I make my favorite coffee. I listen to one of my new favorite songs. I dance around the kitchen. I cry when I remember once again that I can no longer call Momma just to see what she is doing. I read a little. I make note of the growth I am making.

"...He provides for those who grieve – He bestows on them a crown of beauty instead of ashes; the oil of joy instead of mourning, and a garment of praise instead of a spirit of despair."

I "shine my crown of beauty" so to speak.

Picking up my phone to send a reminder to my brother and sister about the 90th birthday party we are planning for our grandmother, I notice some unread messages that I missed earlier that morning. My body tenses. My senses go numb. My freshly shined crown of beauty crumbles into ashes. My world gives way.

Bad news? Death, war, disease? Hunger, tragedy, loss?

Based on my reaction - one would think.

But no. Actually, wonderful news. The kind of news for which people had been praying. The kind of news for which I had been praying. The "God making it happen, coming through, meeting (and exceeding) expectations, doing the thing, showing up" kind of news.

I should be thrilled. I should be praising God. I should be shouting gratitude, adoration, and worship from the rooftops.

Instead, I am crushed. I am battered, marred, bruised, damaged, and beaten.

I am wounded.

A friend of a friend had been battling cancer and received an unexpected clear scan. Not just a scan showing no spread of cancer cells. Not just a scan showing the shrinking of cancerous tumors. A scan showing no cancer at all. A complete healing. God had done it!

The screen on my phone was filled with words like:

"Praise the Lord."

"God is good!"

"All the time."

"Prayer works!"

"Amen, amen, and amen."

All at once, the wound is all I can see. All I can hear, taste, touch, and smell.

Wounded.

Once again, wounded is all I can be.

Why now and not then, God? Why for them and not for us? See, God? You did have a choice. You could have healed her. You could have brought her back to life. You could have done it. You didn't. Why not? What now?

I want to say thank you. I want to live into the gratitude, adoration, and worship that this kind of news deserves. I want to tell God that I am in awe of His power, grace, mercy, and love. But all I can think are the questions.

The same crushing questions with which I have been wrestling for months.

How do I worship you now?

Why not?

What now?

Where is your goodness?

How do I worship you now?

My phone alerts me to another text and I hesitate. I don't want to read it. I'm not sure I can handle one more message praising God for showing up.

I pick up my phone anyway and I am blown away by the words I read. A text just to me, not the group. A text with four simple words.

"I am so sorry."

Another text comes right after.

"This must be hard news for you to take, my friend. We should have gotten to celebrate God's healing of your Momma too. He could have done it. I am so sorry."

Breathe in.

I am not alone.

Breathe out.

Thank you, Jesus.

Wounded is part of me, but wounded is not all of me.

Breathe in. Gratitude.

Thank you for the gift of this moment.

Breathe out. Adoration.

You made this, God. You did this.

Wounded is part of me, but wounded is not all of me. It can be both.

7 the "And If Not"

Time keeps moving. Seconds turn into minutes. Minutes turn into hours. Hours turn into days. Days turn into weeks. Weeks turn into months. And all of a sudden, months have turned into a year. One full year. Twelve months. Fifty-two weeks. Three hundred sixty-five days. Eight thousand seven hundred sixty hours. Five hundred twenty-five thousand six hundred minutes. Thirty-one million five hundred thirty-six thousand seconds.

One year ago today I found myself living out moments that have been permanently seared into my memories. Moments I absolutely hate, yet moments I would have hated even more to have missed.

One year ago today I found myself praying with my family, sitting around my Momma's hospital bed. I found myself whispering into Sweet Momma's ear, speaking words that I desperately wanted her to hear me say one last time. I found myself listening to Momma's favorite worship songs, hoping they would bring peace and comfort to her as her breaths became fewer and farther between. I found myself frantically searching my brother's face as he felt for Sweet Momma's pulse one last time. I found myself almost collapsing as we walked down the hallway away from her room, knowing she would never walk out of it behind us. I found myself driving away from the hospital without my Momma, knowing I wouldn't get to return the next day to visit her again.

Thirty-one million five hundred thirty-six thousand seconds ago I found myself living a part of my story for which I did not ask, nor did I want – the "and if not."

My soul was crushed. I was (and in some ways still am) struggling to comprehend that God had not shown up in the way for which we had begged. I found myself living in the "and if not".

"And if not", unfortunately, is a reality of life. In Daniel 3:17-18, Shadrach, Meshach, and Abednego (just before being thrown into a fiery furnace and, one could only assume, what would be the death sentence for all three men) boldly speak the words, "the God we serve is able to deliver us... And even if He doesn't, we want you to know, Your Majesty, that we will not worship any other gods…"

And even if He does not. And if not.

These men knew God was able, yet they also knew the reality that the "and if not" was possible. And they were willing to worship the Lord, even in the midst of the "and if not".

I'll be honest - as we walked out of the hospital 365 days ago, I was still somewhat convinced that God might show up. He might just want to surprise us all with an even bigger miracle. He could do it! Maybe we are living in the "even now", I hoped, rather than the "and if not".

Even now you have a choice, Lord. You could still heal her. You could still bring her back to life. You could do it… Will you please?

I wanted nothing more than to cling to the "even now".

Even now you have a choice, Lord. You could still heal her. You could still bring her back to life. You could do it… Will you please?

Yet, here we are. One year later. He didn't heal her. He didn't bring her back to life. He didn't do it. We are no longer living in the "even now". We are, in fact, living in the "and if not".

The last year has been filled with questions and doubts,

fear and frailty, sorrow and despair. The "why" and "why not" questions have been common in my daily wrestling matches with God. And to be completely honest with you, my friends - I am simply not satisfied with the answers to those questions. The reality is that we live in a fallen world. Things are not as they should be, nor are they as God intended them to be. Like it or not, at some point trauma and tragedy will bump up against each and every one of us - sometimes from our own doing, but more often than not, it is simply a result of living in a broken world. Loss, sickness, death, and pain are real. So now what?

As I reread the story of Shadrach, Meshach, and Abednego, I am struck by one question. What made them choose God? In their own "and if not", what made them choose to worship?

I think it is because they knew the truth that I am still coming to understand. "Every good and perfect gift is from above, coming down from the Father of the heavenly lights, who does not change like shifting shadows."

"...who does not change like shifting shadows."

Does not change. Help me to see that it is true, God. Help me to worship you now.

If scripture is truly God's word (and I believe it is), and if His word can be trusted (and I believe it can), then I have to believe those words that have been haunting my thoughts.

"...who does not change like shifting shadows."

Does not change. Help me to see that it is true, God. Help me to worship you now.

I have to believe that He does not change. And if He does not change, then I have to believe He truly is for us. He truly does weep with us. He truly does comfort those who mourn. He truly is the God of healing and restoration. And He truly is making all things new.

"...He provides for those who grieve – He bestows on them a crown of beauty instead of ashes; the oil of joy instead of mourning, and a garment of praise instead of a spirit of despair."

Whether He is doing so in the way we would ask or not, He is making all things new. He is.

For the one year anniversary of losing Momma, my family and I have decided to release butterflies in her memory. I can hear the butterflies rustling around in the box, waiting in anticipation for a chance to stretch their wings. The soft sound is surprisingly peaceful and calm, filled with expectation and hope. When we open the paper in which they have been gently wrapped, there is nothing frantic in how the butterflies move. They are tentative. They start slowly, one small movement at a time. They take their time.

As I watch one butterfly in particular, I remember Momma's words.

"Ab, no matter what happens, don't ever forget that God is good. Don't ever forget that He is faithful. And don't ever forget that He is with you always. Everything is going to be ok."

I blink back the tears and smile at her. Even though she isn't physically here, I can feel her in the air. I can almost hear her soothing, encouraging voice in the rustle of the breeze. She knew. She was fully aware of how often I would need to remember those words over the coming seconds, minutes, hours, days, weeks, months, and even years.

Now a full year later, sitting quietly in our backyard, flames dancing in our firepit and lighting the intimate memorial we have created as we release our butterflies, I find myself reliving those minutes in the hospital room. I want to go back to that moment. I want to be in my Momma's kind and encouraging presence. I want to ask her to tell me more. I want her to tell me everything is going to be ok. I want to watch her listen to the music with her eyes closed, her face calm, her hand holding the handmade wooden cross, lovingly made by my brother in law.

I want to ask her how she did it. She was about my age

when cancer took her own mother. In a very similar way, my Sweet Momma lost her best friend, her protector, her confidant, her biggest fan, her momma bear in every sense of the word. Loss, pain, grief, and trauma entered her world, just as it has entered mine, and I want to ask her how she became a wounded worshipper. How did she live in the "and if not"?

But I don't have to ask her.

I know the answer.

She told me.

"Ab, no matter what happens, don't ever forget that God is good. Don't ever forget that He is faithful. And don't ever forget that He is with you always. Everything is going to be ok."

Gratitude. Adoration. Worship.

"Every good and perfect gift is from above, coming down from the Father of the heavenly lights, who does not change like shifting shadows."

"...who does not change like shifting shadows."

Does not change. Help me to see that it is true, God. Help me to worship you now.

God truly is for us. He truly does weep with us. He truly does comfort those who mourn. He truly is the God of healing and restoration. And He truly is making all things new.

"...He provides for those who grieve – He bestows on them a crown of beauty instead of ashes; the oil of joy instead of mourning, and a garment of praise instead of a spirit of despair."

Whether He is doing so in the way we would ask or not, He is making all things new. He is.

Living in the "and if not" means trusting those truths. Living in the "and if not" means learning how to keep moving forward. Living in the "and if not" means learning how to seek and find joy - looking for beauty in the mess.

The butterflies are still dancing around the sweet smelling lemon tree, finding joy in their movement, stretching their wings more and more with each and every flutter. One small movement at a time. They take their time. I see myself in the tentative, yet hope-filled rustle of their wings.

At least I want to see myself.

My heart is not fully healed. My pain and grief are not over. But after a year of missing my Momma in the very depths of my being, I want to worship.

At least I want to want to worship.

I want to join Shadrach, Meshach, and Abednego in

their response to the "and if not".

At least I want to want to join Shadrach, Meshach, and Abednego in their response to the "and if not".

One year ago today began my journey with the hardest "and if not" I've ever experienced. God did not show up as I had hoped, imagined, or begged. My "even now" prayers turned into the "and if not" kind of prayers. But Momma was right. I have to believe that she was right.

"Ab, no matter what happens, don't ever forget that God is good. Don't ever forget that He is faithful. And don't ever forget that He is with you always. Everything is going to be ok."

Gratitude. Adoration. Worship.

"Every good and perfect gift is from above, coming down from the Father of the heavenly lights, who does not change like shifting shadows."

"...who does not change like shifting shadows."

Does not change. Help me to see that it is true, God. Help me to worship you now.

God truly is for us. He truly does weep with us. He truly does comfort those who mourn. He truly is the God of healing and restoration. And He truly is making all things new.

"...He provides for those who grieve – He bestows on

them a crown of beauty instead of ashes; the oil of joy instead of mourning, and a garment of praise instead of a spirit of despair."

Whether He is doing so in the way we would ask or not, He is making all things new. He is.

One year ago today began my journey with the hardest "and if not" I've ever experienced. And still, I will choose to worship the Lord. And even if He doesn't. And if not. I will choose to worship.

The butterflies are still dancing around the sweet smelling lemon tree, finding joy in their movement, stretching their wings more and more with each and every flutter. One small movement at a time. They take their time.

I see myself in the tentative, yet hope-filled rustle of their wings. I do. I am becoming a wounded worshipper.

Breathe in.

I am not alone.

Breathe out.

Thank you, Jesus.

Breathe in. Gratitude.

Thank you for the gift of this moment.

Breathe out. Adoration.

You made this, God. You did this.

Wounded is part of me, but wounded is not all of me. It can be both.

8 And Yet

It is Christmas again. I am sitting in the sanctuary of our church. Warm smelling pine trees, alive with twinkling lights, stand proudly in every corner of the stage. The band is made up of beautiful souls whom I consider to be friends. The music sounds hauntingly familiar. The air is filled with the sweet voices of those standing around me. And the words... The words make sense in a way that they never have before.

"O come, O come, Emmanuel

And ransom captive Israel

That mourns in lonely exile here

Until the Son of God appear..."

I find myself, yet again, unable to fight back the tears.

O come, Emmanuel. I am mourning. I am lonely. In many ways, grief has made me feel like I am in exile. O come.

"Disperse the gloomy clouds of night

And death's dark shadows put to flight…"

The words cut straight to the heart of my woundedness.

O come, Emmanuel. Death has left such dark shadows. Bring light. Clear the clouds that grief has cast over my days. O come.

"Rejoice! Rejoice! Emmanuel

Shall come to thee O Israel…"

I can no longer resist the truth. I am becoming a wounded worshipper.

You have not left me alone in my grief. You have come. Thank you, sweet Jesus. Emmanuel. Thank you for showing up.

Most days I don't want to admit my ability to worship again, because I am worried someone might think I am over it. I have this fear that people will think I am all better. I don't want the world to view me as being done with grief.

"O come, O come, Emmanuel

And ransom captive Israel

That mourns in lonely exile here

Until the Son of God appear...

Disperse the gloomy clouds of night

And death's dark shadows put to flight...

Rejoice! Rejoice! Emmanuel

Shall come to thee O Israel..."

As the precious lyrics become my guttural cry to God, I recognize the undeniable reality - I am becoming a wounded worshipper.

I am not over it.

I am not all better.

I am not done with grief.

And yet, I cry out to God. I choose to worship.

I've been thinking a lot lately about that night, seemingly a lifetime ago, when I stood confidently in that old movie theater turned sanctuary and spoke about worship. And I continue to ask myself - would I stand on that stage again? Are the words I spoke still true? Where do I stand now - now that I am wounded?

My understanding of worship has always been grounded in my belief that God loves us completely. He is utterly delighted by us. And He has given us grace, mercy, and love. My ability and desire to worship has always been secured in my belief that God sent His Son for our sakes. He did not leave us alone. And we have direct access to love and grace because He showed up.

But what about now? Is my understanding of worship still grounded now that I am wounded? Is my worship still secured? Do I still mean every single word? Are those beliefs still true?

It has been a hard road to get to the point where I can confidently say yes. But, as I cry out to God through the words of that hauntingly familiar carol, I find that I have no other answer. Yes. Still grounded, still secured, still absolutely true. In the midst of death's dark shadows, yes.

God loves us completely.

I am not over it.

I am not all better.

I am not done with grief.

And yet, You still love me completely, God. I choose to worship.

God is utterly delighted by us.

I am not over it.

I am not all better.

I am not done with grief.

And yet, You are still utterly delighted by me, God. I choose to worship.

God has given us grace, mercy, and love.

I am not over it.

I am not all better.

I am not done with grief.

And yet, You have given me grace, mercy, and love, God. I choose to worship.

God sent His Son for our sakes.

I am not over it.

I am not all better.

I am not done with grief.

And yet, You sent Your Son for my sake, God. I choose to worship.

God did not leave us alone.

I am not over it.

I am not all better.

I am not done with grief.

And yet, You did not leave me alone, God. I choose to worship.

We have direct access to love and grace because God showed up.

I am not over it.

I am not all better.

I am not done with grief.

And yet, I have direct access to love and grace because You showed up, God. I choose to worship.

"O come, O come, Emmanuel

And ransom captive Israel

That mourns in lonely exile here

Until the Son of God appear…

Disperse the gloomy clouds of night

And death's dark shadows put to flight…

Rejoice! Rejoice! Emmanuel

Shall come to thee O Israel…"

The tears continue to flow. The precious lyrics my guttural cry to God.

Rejoice! Rejoice! Emmanuel came for me…

I am not over it.

I am not all better.

I am not done with grief.

And yet, I cry out to You, God. I choose to worship.

9 Practicing

Nothing about grief is linear. The idea of making it through specific stages and moving forward does not give a helpful picture of the journey those who are grieving must walk. There are no clear steps. There are no specific paths laid out. There are no clean cut timelines. Seemingly infinite words can be used to describe grief, but linear is simply not one of them.

So much time has passed, but so often I continue to find myself sitting with clenched fists. My muscles tightened. My body full of tension, pain, anger, fear, worry, doubt, despair, and sadness.

Then those same words that were providing such melodic accompaniment to the butterflies dancing in my side yard begin to replay in my mind.

"...who does not change like shifting shadows."

I breathe. Eyes close.

I breathe. Muscles release.

I breathe. Hands open.

I breathe. Mind focuses.

I will myself to consider the gifts in my life. Where is beauty, even in the mess? Where is hope, even in the despair? Where is life, even in the pain? Where is love, even in the mourning?

I breathe. Eyes close. Where is beauty, even in the mess?

There is beauty in the flowers growing outside my window.

I breathe. Muscles release. Where is hope, even in the despair?

There is hope in the music playing on the radio.

I breathe. Hands open. Where is life, even in the pain?

There is life in the laughter of my children.

I breathe. Mind focuses. Where is love, even in the mourning?

There is love in the note my husband left for me this morning.

This becomes my practice. Some days I forget. Some days I resist. Some days I fail miserably. But this becomes my practice. I am relearning how to practice worship. I am becoming a wounded worshipper.

Gratitude. Adoration. Worship.

I breathe. Eyes close.

There is beauty in the sunset I watched during my evening walk yesterday.

I breathe. Muscles release.

There is hope in the book I am currently reading.

I breathe. Hands open.

There is life in the precious baby born to my sweet friend last week.

I breathe. Mind focuses.

There is love in the stories we share over dinner as a family.

This practice becomes more natural. A part of how I move through my days. Some days I still forget. Some days I still resist. Some days I still fail miserably. But this practice becomes more natural. I am practicing worship. I am a wounded worshipper.

Gratitude. Adoration. Worship.

I breathe. Eyes close.

There is beauty in the photo my sister texted of the mountains near her home.

I breathe. Muscles release.

There is hope in the conversation I had with my counselor this afternoon.

I breathe. Hands open.

There is life in the hilarious phone call I had with my brother tonight.

I breathe. Mind focuses.

There is love in the memories my dad shares about Sweet Momma.

This natural practice becomes part of who I am. A part of how I view the world around me. Some days I still forget. Some days I still resist. Some days I still fail miserably. But this natural practice becomes part of who I am.

"...who does not change like shifting shadows."

I breathe. Eyes close. Where is beauty, even in the mess?

I breathe. Muscles release. Where is hope, even in the despair?

I breathe. Hands open. Where is life, even in the pain?

I breathe. Mind focuses. Where is love, even in the mourning?

Nothing about grief is linear, but I am practicing worship.

10 A New Perspective

Growing up, I remember hearing multiple sermons and devotions on offering our bodies as an act of worship. I remember being told that it is important to refrain from "things of this world" that would not be considered holy or pleasing to God. And I do believe it is important to seek personal holiness and right living. Learning to live with healthy restraint is good.

But as I reread the scripture upon which these teachings are based, I find myself seeing a new perspective. A new angle, so to speak.

"Therefore, I urge you, brothers and sisters, in view of God's mercy, to offer your bodies as a living sacrifice, holy and pleasing to God - this is your true and proper worship." Romans 12:1

In view of God's mercy... Offer your bodies...

I begin to consider - what mercies have I experienced? Each and every thing I have been given in my life is a mercy. A gift. A grace. And if each of those blessings is from God, which I believe it is, what should my response be? Offer my body. But how?

God created us to experience the world through our senses. We hear, smell, see, taste, and touch every single moment. And each of those sensory moments gives us a chance to respond. A chance to offer our sensory experiences as an act of worship.

Gratitude. Adoration. Worship.

I hear such lovely harmonies being sung by the birds today. You did this, God. Thank you for the gift of sound.

I smell such comforting notes of citrus in the simmer on my stove today. You did this, God. Thank you for the gift of smell.

I see such beautiful clouds in the sky today. You did this, God. Thank you for the gift of sight.

I taste such sweet and complex flavors in the dark chocolate I ate today. You did this, God. Thank you for the gift of taste.

I feel such a soft breeze in the air today. You did this, God. Thank you for the gift of touch.

Moments become etched in our bodies through our senses. We can choose to respond with gratitude, adoration, and worship as we experience such sensations. Or not.

A new perspective. A new angle.

When God gives me the gift of a moment, filled with a multitude of sensations that become etched in my body through the sounds, smells, sights, tastes, and textures I experience, how do I respond?

Gratitude. Adoration. Worship.

In view of God's mercy... Offer your bodies...

The waves of grief blindside me in the most unexpected times and places. My woundedness remains a constant part of me. The practice of responding with worship is becoming more natural as the days continue, but loss is ever present.

I have found a truth in my woundedness. Losing one gift does not negate the others that remain. Wounded is a part of me, but wounded is not all of me.

The memories. The stories. The sounds, smells, sights, tastes, and textures I have experienced over the years - even the ones I have experienced due to the gift (and loss) of Sweet Momma - remain a part of me. The sensory moments I have been gifted remain inscribed in my body.

And I can choose to respond with worship. Or not.

When I hear a song from the Cruisin' Classics tape that we used to have the most ridiculous dance parties to when my brother and sister and I were little, I can choose to respond with worship. Or not.

I remember the countless hours we spent dancing to these songs. I miss hearing her laugh as we sang at the top of our lungs and danced until we collapsed breathlessly on the couch. You did that, God. Thank you for the gift of sound.

When I smell the scent of the perfume she used to wear, I can choose to respond with worship. Or not.

I remember closing my eyes as she would hug me when we arrived in the driveway for a visit, breathing in the familiar scent of the perfume she had worn since before I could remember. I miss those fragrant hugs that welcomed me home each and every time. You did that, God. Thank you for the gift of smell.

When I see her favorite flowers blooming in someone else's yard, I can choose to respond with worship. Or not.

I remember how excited she would be when her hydrangeas and ditch lilies would start to bloom each year, calling me to describe the depth of colors and hues she could see from her kitchen window. I miss those phone calls and the tender care she patiently gave to the plants in her yard. You did that, God. Thank you for the gift of sight.

When I taste her wassail recipe that she lovingly made each fall and winter, I can choose to respond with worship. Or not.

I remember her generously offering a cup of hot wassail to any of our friends and family who happened to walk through the door on a cold winter day. I miss her readiness to sip those flavors and calmly listen with such kindness, wisdom, compassion, and love. You did that, God. Thank you for the gift of taste.

When I feel the warmth and comfort of the blanket she so expertly crocheted, I can choose to respond with worship. Or not.

I remember her laying with me on the couch in the sunroom, sharing this same blanket, encouraging me to pursue my dreams and trust in God's goodness. I miss the way she made me feel important, known, and loved. You did that, God. Thank you for the gift of touch.

In view of God's mercy... Offer your bodies...

We know that worship, in its simplest definition, is the expression of reverence and adoration.

Reverence and Adoration. I would venture to say every single one of us on this planet we call Earth has felt reverence and adoration for someone or something. A feeling of awe. A moment in which our very breath has been taken away.

Reverence and adoration are inspired in our very beings by so many different sensations, and I truly believe God intentionally placed that ability to worship within us. He gave us those feelings, and the desire to express them, on purpose.

The question is, what do we do with that ability to worship? When the sounds, smells, sights, tastes, and textures bring us to our knees in reverence and adoration, how do we respond? Do we express our reverence and adoration to the giver of the good things? Or do we express our reverence and adoration to the good things themselves?

"Every good and perfect gift is from above, coming down from the Father of the heavenly lights, who does not change like shifting shadows." James 1:17

The natural progression of worship should be to recognize that each breathtaking moment I experience is a gift. The hug, the fragrance, the sunrise, the melodies, the spices… all a gift, yes. But a gift that, in and of itself, is not worthy of my worship. The giver of that gift - my heavenly Father - He absolutely IS worthy of my worship.

And when the center of those moments revolves around someone or something that has been lost… When the wound becomes so deep that the wound is all I can be… I can sit in the pain of the wound, focusing on the lost gift. Or I can see the gifts that remain. I can remember.

I can choose to remember God's mercy in giving me those moments to begin with.

In view of God's mercy... Offer your bodies...

Gratitude. Adoration. Worship.

I heard such funny jokes from my children today. You did that, God. Thank you for the gift of sound.

I smelled such sweet fragrances from the roses on my way to the car today. You did that, God. Thank you for the gift of smell.

I saw such kind smiles on the faces of my friends today. You did that, God. Thank you for the gift of sight.

I tasted such delicious spices in the global table meal we made as a family today. You did that, God. Thank you for the gift of taste.

I felt such comfort and encouragement in the hug from my husband today. You did that, God. Thank you for the gift of touch.

Moments become etched in our bodies through our senses. We can choose to respond with gratitude, adoration, and worship as we experience such sensations. Or not.

A new perspective. A new angle.

In view of God's mercy... Offer your bodies...

11 I am. I will.

Sitting in the cozy, cherry-brown chair nestled in the corner of my bedroom, I notice the chair's oversized and accepting arms - almost hugging me as I sit. The soft gray of the walls bringing calm to my nervous self. My tiny little seven pound dog is snuggled up in my lap, providing warmth, support, and a much needed sense of belonging. Yet the blank screen in front of me becomes a blindingly white page of unknown. I take a deep breath. I am determined to finish this assignment. I need to finish this assignment.

This is not an assignment given to me by a teacher or professor. This is not an assignment required in order to complete a line of coursework. This is not an assignment recommended to me by some sort of professional in my life, such as my counselor or pastor. This is an assignment given to me by a friend. A sweet friend who is a vital part of my inner circle. A loyal friend who has refused to let me grieve alone. A precious friend who has refused to let me isolate and turn inward on this journey of relearning how to worship. A friend who, in quite tangible ways, has been a lifeline for me.

(Sidenote: Who is in your inner circle, my friends? Find your people. Seek out your lifelines. Be a lifeline for others. We all, every single one of us, desperately need friends who refuse to let us stand alone. Find those friends. Be that friend.)

This dear friend of mine and I were talking a few weeks ago. I told her I have been thinking a lot about my identity lately. What is it that defines me? Who am I? So much of life seems to have changed. Loss and grief have changed me. Can I still be me? After all that has happened? I told her that, in some ways, it is as if loss has stolen my identity. With the loss of Sweet Momma came a loss of self. In very strange, yet very real ways, I have struggled to remember who I am.

Her response was simple. "Then write it down."

Write it down?

"Write it down. Remember. Who are you? Write it down."

Looking around the room, I will myself to remember.

I am a wife, married to my favorite human being on the face of the planet.

I am a mother, charged with the great responsibility to love and care for three amazing children.

I am a sister, the middle of three siblings.

I am a daughter, gifted with the most wonderful, Godly, loving, and encouraging parents.

Remember. What is true about you? Write it down.

I have blonde hair, which gets cut into a pixie cut about once every two or three years.

I have blue eyes, a lot like my Momma's. I have always been proud of having her eyes.

I have more clothes than I need, mostly a mash-up of comfort meets fashion meets budget.

I have tattoos, each one representing a deep reminder that I need to see every single day.

My list is slowly growing. Remember. What makes you "you"? Write it down.

I am a musician. I sing. I play the harp and piano. I own a guitar that I never learned to play.

I am a dancer. I find freedom in movement and rhythm.

I am a teacher. I find joy in helping someone learn a new concept or skill.

I am a writer. Repetition, words on a page, endless revisions and edits. Writing is healing for me.

Remember. What describes you? Write it down.

I have a serious sweet tooth, especially for dark chocolate and salted caramel.

I have a love for cute animals, especially my tiny little emotional support chihuahua.

I have a soft spot for live theater, especially musicals with dancing (bonus points for tap dance).

I have a fear of creepy crawly creatures, especially snakes and spiders.

The surface truths begin to lead to deeper truths. Remember. Who are you? Write it down.

I am a beloved daughter of the Most High.

I am beautifully and wonderfully made.

I am part of a bigger story.

I am loved, adored, needed.

Remember. What matters to you? Write it down.

I have friends and family who refuse to let me stand alone, offering hope and truth every day.

I have precious memories that bring laughter and tears, sometimes both at the same time.

I have a story that is mine to tell. A story that cannot be lived or told by anyone but me.

I have value to bring to the world around me, unique gifts and talents given specifically to me.

Remember. Who are you? Write it down.

I am wounded.

I am hopeful.

I am standing.

I am joyful.

Remember. Who are you? Write it down.

I am me.

I am loved.

I am saved.

I am His.

So much has changed. I have changed. But I am still me. Remember. Who are you? Write it down.

I will worship.

I will live.

I will love my husband and hug my kids.

I will visit my brother and sister.

I will check in on my dad.

I will remember my Momma.

I will grow my hair out, braid it, ponytail it, and likely even chop it off into a cute pixie again.

I will wear cute clothes.

I will get more tattoos.

I will play more songs, dance more dances, teach more lessons, write more words.

I will eat more dark chocolate and salted caramel.

I will laugh at more jokes, jump away from more spiders, make more memories, tell more stories.

I will stand in my woundedness with hope and joy.

So much has changed. I have changed. But I am still me. I will worship.

12 Remember

I am wounded. I am healing. I am a worshipper.

As I continue to heal though, I have found myself nervous. Anxious. Scared.

I am asking new questions now.

What if I forget? What if I wake up one morning and I can't remember her? What if I am unable to recall the moments that have etched themselves into my very being? What if I forget my Sweet Momma? What if I can't remember my best friend?

The memories. The stories. The good. The bad. The everything. There are things I just don't want to forget. There are things I want to remember. There are things I have to remember.

I decide to write this down, too. A new assignment - given to myself, from myself.

Remember. Who was she? Write it down.

Another blindingly white blank screen stares me down, taunting me with the pressure to get the words just right. And I simply cannot find them. The words seem to be stuck deep within my being. I know them. I think them. But I am paralyzed. My fingers are frozen. I cannot put them to the task.

Remember. Who was she? Write it down.

Hesitantly, I open a file on my computer. A file I have avoided recently. A file I know completely, but haven't viewed in months. A file titled, "once a mother." I haven't read these words since my first Mother's Day without Sweet Momma. I wrote them months before that though. I wrote them for Momma. I printed them out and spoke them at her funeral. I spoke them on that day. The day. The day my wounding became real.

As the file slowly opens on my old, slowly working laptop, my breath catches in my lungs. I need to read these words. I need to remember.

> "As I thought about what to share today, I found myself unsure of where to begin. There is so much to say about the most amazing woman. I could share about Momma's faith. Or how she served

others. I could share about how she always had time to care for and listen to her kids. Or how she had a way of making each and every person who walked into her life feel loved and special. I could share about her legacy, her marriage to my sweet Daddy, the family she built, or the void we feel now that she is no longer here on this earth with us.

I'll be honest. Though there are thousands upon thousands of words to be said in order to express the beauty that was our Momma, I find myself somewhat at a loss for words. I miss my Sweet Momma... I miss my friend... I miss everything about her.

So I have decided to simply share something I wrote for Momma while she was in the hospital. Something that shares one of the countless ways in which she will be missed. Something that I already miss.

Once a mother, always a mother...

One of the phrases I remember hearing most from Momma, other than 'I love you', was 'once a mother, always a mother.' I will so miss hearing her say those words to me.

Momma didn't just say those words. She lived them... in such beautiful (and sometimes frustrating) ways.

I remember being about 13 years old. Momma would drive me over to Louisville for music lessons and rehearsals multiple times each week. And at least once a week, she would see a car down the street, usually about three lights away, and she would slam her arm in front of me to make sure I was not about to cross the street yet. I'd give her that look that only teenage girls can give, and say, 'Mom, I've got it.'

She'd return my look with that look that only moms of teenage girls can give, and say,

'I know, Ab. But once a mother, always a mother. I love you.'

In high school, as I would get ready to leave the house for whatever rehearsal, performance, or class was on the schedule for that day, she'd always ask me if I had everything I needed. She would ask about each individual item. Homework. Yes, Mom. Change of clothes for rehearsal. Yes, Mom. Dance shoes. Yes, Mom. Costumes. Yes, Mom. Snacks so you don't get hungry. Yes, Mom.

And as soon as she could tell I was beginning to get impatient, I'd hear those words.

'I know, Ab. But once a mother, always a mother. I love you.'

In college, as I would be driving the three hours back to school, she would ask me to call her to let her know I made it safely. And inevitably I would forget to call. But somehow she would always know when I'd been back for about 30 minutes. I would hear the phone ring, and I wouldn't even have to say hello when I answered. I always knew it was her.

'Hi Momma. Sorry I didn't call. I'm safe.'

'I know, Ab. But once a mother, always a mother. I love you.'

On the day I became a mother myself, after giving birth to our oldest, Momma came into the birthing room to check on me. Through tears I said, 'I did it, Momma. I did it.'

She smiled, kissed me, and said, 'I know, Ab. I knew you could. I'm so proud of you. Now it's your turn. Once a mother, always a mother. I love you.'

Momma would find ways to love on all of us every single day. Phone calls. Texts. Packages. Cards. Frozen meals for the crockpot. Keeping our kiddos. Hosting holidays. Organizing anything and everything we would let her get her hands on. The list is unending. And her reasoning was always, 'once a mother, always a mother. I love you.'

Even when she was in the hospital with fevers, pain, and low oxygen levels, she would try to kick me out around 4pm every day. She would say, 'You get home before it gets dark and you get stuck in traffic.'

I'd give her that look that only worried daughters can give, and say, 'Mom, I've got it.'

She'd return my look with that look that only loving mommas can give.

'I know, Ab. But once a mother, always a mother. I love you.'

Momma, I will forever miss hearing you say those words to me. And I know you told me that I can do this. That we can do this. That you're ok and that we've got it. And you're right. I know, Momma. But once a daughter, always a daughter. I miss you so, so terribly. I love you."

Once a mother, always a mother.

Oh, how I wish I could hear her say those words to me one more time. I didn't just write about those words. Or speak those words at her funeral. I live those words.

Every single day. I now know what she meant when she spoke them. I know what she felt when she lived them. I just wish I could hear her say them again.

Once a mother, always a mother.

Remember. Who was she? Write it down.

The tears are flowing, and the words begin to pour out now - faster than my fingers can keep up.

Remember. Who was she? Write it down.

Momma was a mere five feet tall standing next to Daddy's commanding stature of six feet four inches. She was tiny, but don't let her size fool you. She was our momma bear. Fierce. Isn't that something Shakespere said? "Though she be but little, she is fierce." That was our Sweet Momma.

Momma always had time. And space. Or maybe it wasn't that she had both time and space. Looking back, I realize that she made both time and space.

When she was cooking–

"Come help me."

When she was reading–

"Come snuggle with me."

When she was getting ready to go out–

"Come talk to me."

When she was working on a cross stitch project, mending a hem, writing a thank you card or get-well note to someone, eating out with friends, shopping, you name it–

"I'm here for you. Tell me. What's up, babe?"

She always made both time and space.

"Don't let your Saturday night affect your Sunday morning." How many times did my teenage self hear those words?

Remember. Who was she? Write it down.

Momma loved Daddy. Fully. Mom and Dad lived such a beautiful love story. They were each other's biggest fans. They enjoyed each other's company. They saw each other, learned about and from each other, served each other. In Momma's final days, Daddy read to Momma every night. After my brother, sister, and I would leave the hospital for the night, Daddy would settle in. He'd pull his chair closer to Sweet Momma, gently grasp her hand, and gaze at his beautiful bride. He would take out notes he had written, cards others had sent, his Bible, anything else that might mean something to her. Adjusting his glasses, Daddy would spend the evening reading words of love. What a love story. What an example. What a gift.

Momma was involved. She made sure we knew she was interested and cared. She gave of her time and talents for us. If I was in a show, she would organize ticket sales. If my brother was in a soccer tournament, she would coordinate travel and meals. If my sister was studying abroad, she would visit and send care packages. I could fill page after page of how Sweet Momma showed up. Class mom, PTO president, VBS teacher, file organizer, nail painter, outfit ironer, stain remover, hug giver, tear catcher, shoulder to cry on, wisdom giver, spirit lifter... so many things in so many ways. She showed up. I miss that. I want to do that. I want to be that.

Momma liked to laugh. She loved deeply. She cared about her family and her friends. Her love language was one hundred percent acts of service. She would do for others, without hesitation. She cooked. She crafted. She organized. She called, texted, emailed, and sent cards. She traveled, experienced cultures, saw humanity, prayed unceasingly, studied God's word, and generously gave of herself.

Remember. Who was she? Write it down.

Momma loved music. She always wanted to have a beautiful voice. She would say that Jesus was going to give her a "new voice" when she made it to heaven. We played music during her time at the hospital. A lot. She wanted good words to be in her thoughts and on our lips, even in her final moments. As we sat around her hospital bed, we held hands. We prayed. We sang. We took deep breaths. We listened. We cried. We held our breath. We frantically searched each other's faces for hope. We let good words bring comfort, even as we heard her breath disappear. The last six songs she heard on this earth, before going home to heaven and receiving her "new voice", were some of her favorites.

"How Great Thou Art" performed by Carrie Underwood

"So Will I" performed by Hillsong

"It Is Well" performed by Audrey Assad

"Worn" performed by Tenth Avenue North

"Amazing Grace" performed by BYU Noteworthy

"You Raise Me Up" performed by Selah

I miss her love of music. I miss her earthly voice. I wonder what her "new voice" sounds like. I'm sure it is absolutely breathtaking and awe-inspiring… beautiful, just like her.

Remember. Who was she? Write it down.

Momma was wounded. Tragedy and heartache were not strangers. She fought her own battles with woundedness. And yet, she stood in her woundedness with joy and hope. Wounded was a part of her, but wounded was not all of her.

Momma was a worshipper.

Remember. Who was she? Write it down.

Momma was beautiful. Momma was a wounded worshipper. Momma was a beautiful wounded worshipper.

13 this Side of Heaven

As I step out of the car, my borrowed boots hitting the cold, black pavement, I realize I have been holding my breath since the moment I took the left turn into the entrance. My heart has been beating faster than normal since the moment I took the second left onto the pathway that leads toward my destination. My hands have been shaking since the moment the courtyard and building came into view. I haven't been back here in over two years.

Taking a step toward the door, the heel of my boot clicks louder than it should. I stop in my tracks and quickly look down. Not knowing what it is that I am expecting, I hold my breath. Yet nothing extraordinary has happened. Nothing is out of the ordinary or significant about the sound of the heels on the hard ground. Except that they still aren't actually my heels. They are still her heels. More than two years later, and they still don't feel like mine. More than two years later, and they still feel borrowed. More than two years later, and I still don't want them. I still don't want this. I still don't want to be here – hearing these sounds, smelling these smells, feeling these feelings, doing these things. I still don't want anything to do with this.

But I didn't get a choice. Not in this.

But you did, God. You did have a choice. You could have healed her, Lord. But you didn't. And yet, I choose to trust You. And yet, I choose to worship. Wounded and worshipping.

I take a few more steps toward the door and I remember that day when I caught my brother's eye. My baby brother. Larger than life, his tears freely flowing down. Five of his closest friends stood with him. The beautifully carved wooden box between them. 1, 2, 3, lift. It is as if I can see them in action once again. The weight of the entire world resting on my brother's shoulders. On all of our shoulders. I remember watching him intensely as the quiet processional carried the casket indoors. I could see it in his eyes. Our thoughts were identical.

As I am about to step through the door, I remember that day when I felt my sister grasp my fingers. My big sister. Our fashionable and fearless leader, with her hands desperate for something to hold. I remember gazing at her profile as she stared down the task before us. I could see it in her shoulders. She, my rock solid sister, was thinking the exact same thoughts.

More than two years later, and still, none of us want this. None of us want anything to do with this.

But we didn't get a choice. Not in this.

But you did, God. You did have a choice. You could have healed her, Lord. But you didn't. And yet, I choose to trust You. And yet, I choose to worship. Wounded and worshipping.

The key to the mausoleum has been on my keyring for the past two years: a constant reminder of these doors and this place. As I slip the key into the door, my breath catches. I see her name before I even turn the key. The wind picks up. The brown leaves on the ground blow past me. The world outside of the cemetery is unknowingly continuing forward with their daily routines and to do lists. And I stand here. Frozen to the spot. Wearing my borrowed boots. Willing myself to turn the key and open the door... unable to do so quite yet.

After a few moments of staring at her name, knowing it would be there yet still shocked to see it staring back at me, I step through the doors. The mausoleum is still. Disturbingly quiet. There are no friends and family to stand alongside me this time. I am alone. And nothing about this moment feels welcoming or calm.

I stand just a few steps into the room and aimlessly look

around me. I allow my eyes to rest on her name again. The year of her death so nonchalantly staring back at me. Callously and unwaveringly real. Reminding me of the finality of death this side of heaven.

Her cute little heeled boots are unable to do their job. They can no longer keep my knees from buckling underneath me. I can't stand any longer and my breath becomes difficult to catch. My heart simultaneously beats out of my chest and seems to simply stop mid-beat.

Those words ring loudly in my ears, as though someone has begun saying them over surround sound speakers. This side of heaven. Over and over they play. Audible only to me.

This side of heaven. This side of heaven. This side of heaven.

I take a deep breath.

This side of the beautiful gift of heaven.

Breathe in. Breathe out.

The gift of heaven.

Another slow, intentional breath.

Heaven.

I sit on the floor, not caring if anyone sees me lacking

every single bit of decorum and grace. I cross my legs, place my head and hands on the cold granite slab that seals my Sweet Momma's casket into the wall, and the tears begin to flow. Uncontrollable, guttural, heart wrenching sobs wrack my body. More than two years later, and the loss is still so achingly deep.

I still don't want this. I still don't want to be here – hearing these sounds, smelling these smells, feeling these feelings, doing these things. I still don't want anything to do with this.

But I didn't get a choice. Not in this.

But you did, God. You did have a choice. You could have healed her, Lord. But you didn't. And yet, I choose to trust You. And yet, I choose to worship. Wounded and worshipping.

As my weeping begins to subside, my breath begins to calm, and my heartbeat begins to normalize. I begin to talk. I talk to my Momma first. I know she isn't actually there. She is in heaven. She has received the beautiful gift of heaven. My head knows this fully, but my heart still needs her to hear me. It has been a long time since I have let myself talk to her. I need to tell her all of the things.

"I miss you, Sweet Momma. We all do. Every single day. But, oh! You would be so proud of your grandkids. They are amazing. You would shake your head so much at all of us, though. You'd be laughing and keeping us in line all at the same time. I am still a bit of a hot mess, Momma. My organization skills haven't quite taken hold just yet. But I try. I still love hard and feel deeply. And I mess up a lot. I am trying so hard. I am learning how to live without you here. We all are. The new normal is still very unwelcome, but it feels less foreign than it did. Some days are harder than others. I still pick up my phone to call you or text you. I still think about how much I need your advice and encouragement. I still wonder how you did this with such grace and beauty. I can honestly say, Momma – I do choose to trust God. I do choose to worship Him. I am wounded and worshipping. Thank you for teaching me how to be both. I didn't know how much strength it took for you to be the mom you were. Thank you. I miss you. I love you. Thank you."

I sit in silence for a while. I'm not sure how long I have been staring at the floor, my head resting on her wall. I look up and focus my eyes on her name again. The year of her death is still staring back at me. Still reminding me of the finality of death that is this side of heaven. I place my hands on the smooth wall.

This side of heaven.

I take a deep breath.

This side of the beautiful gift of heaven.

Breathe in. Breathe out.

The gift of heaven.

Another slow, intentional breath.

Heaven.

God, I really did fully believe you would do it. I truly believed that you would heal her. Every fiber of my being was certain of it. But you didn't. I still don't understand. I still wish I had more time with my precious Momma.

Silence. I take a few deep breaths.

But God, you did give me the gift of her. For the amount of time she was here, she was an absolute gift. Her memory is a gift. Her legacy is a gift. Her wisdom and example – amazing gifts. She remains such a lovely gift.

Breathe in.

You gave me the gift of Sweet Momma.

Breathe out.

Thank you, Jesus.

Wounded is part of me, but wounded is not all of me.

Breathe in. Gratitude.

Thank you for the gift of her.

Breathe out. Adoration.

You did that, God.

Wounded is part of me, but wounded is not all of me. It can be both.

I wish I could have more time, God. And yet, I choose to trust You. And yet, I choose to worship. Wounded and worshipping.

The tears have started flowing again. I look at my hands resting on the wall. They resemble her hands. I used to love watching her hands. Her slender fingers. The slight tremor in her movements. The graceful way in which she would touch the world around her with such beauty, compassion, kindness, and love. The reassuring way in which she would help me know that everything was going to be ok.

As I stare at my hands, I remember her words from that day in the hospital.

"Ab, no matter what happens, don't ever forget that God is good. Don't ever forget that He is faithful. And don't ever forget that He is with you always. Everything is going to be okay."

I muster the rest of my strength and stand. I look at her name one more time. What a gift you were, Momma. What a gift you continue to be.

This side of heaven.

I take a deep breath.

This side of the beautiful gift of heaven.

Breathe in. Breathe out.

The gift of heaven.

Another slow, intentional breath.

Heaven.

I turn to walk out the door. To the sunshine. To the clouds. To the people God has given me to love. To the good, the bad, the ups and the downs. To the beautiful world in which we live.

Gratitude. Adoration. Worship.

Life is filled with so much hard, Lord. I don't understand all of it. I know I never will. And yet, I choose to trust You. And yet, I choose to worship. Wounded and worshipping.

Epilogue

Grief is a strange process, my friends. Grieving is difficult and ugly. But isn't it beautiful as well? Loss is inevitable, but what a sad world it would be if we never loved someone or something enough to truly grieve.

The world is filled with analogies that try to explain the grief journey. A spiral. Stages. A staircase. Confetti. Waves. A box with a button. Living with an amputation. The descriptions and analogies are endless. The truth is grief is all of those things, and it never goes away. Ever. It changes. It morphs. It surprises you and catches you off guard in the most inopportune of moments. And yet, in an odd way, grief becomes a familiar companion. An inseparable piece of who you have become.

It has been quite awhile since Sweet Momma took her final breaths this side of heaven. I have learned so much through my grief journey, but I am also well aware that my grief is not over. The learning is not complete. My journey is in no way done.

Triggers of grief are unexpected and sudden. New loss and sorrow have, and will continue to come my way. Moments of life will knock the wind out of my sails, so to speak. And maybe that is one of the biggest things I have learned. We each have our own timelines with grief. And that timeline is in no way linear. Never be ashamed to walk your journey, dear souls. Sit with the sad and the pain. Relish the memories. Soak up the joy. Stand with hope. Dance when you can dance. Cry when you need to cry. Laugh and smile as often as possible. Be honest about your journey.

Remember: yes, grieving is difficult and ugly, and yet it is oh so beautiful as well. What a sad world it would be if we never loved someone or something enough to truly grieve.

Love you infinity, Momma. I miss you. Still not a day goes by that I don't wish I could call you just to see what you're doing.

Journal Prompts

CHAPTER 1 / EVEN NOW

What is a moment in your life in which you didn't have a choice?

How did you ask God to intervene?

When have you found yourself saying, "Why not, God? What now?"

CHAPTER 2 / WOUNDED

What, in your woundedness, do you do simply because you can?

Or not do, because you don't have to?

What questions do you not ask God because you don't want to know the answer?

CHAPTER 3 / NOT ALONE

Describe the moments in which God's goodness has been hard to find.

What places used to feel safe, but in grief have become foreign to you?

Is it possible you are not alone?

CHAPTER 4 / TWO TRUTHS

What are your truths in grief?

Do you feel alone?

Do you want to be alone?

Is it possible you are not alone?

Think about that feeling – something kind of like gratitude.

What sparks even the slightest moment of something close to gratitude for you?

CHAPTER 5 / WORDS ON THE PAGE

How has your world changed?

Does it seem God has changed as well? How?

CHAPTER 6 / IT CAN BE BOTH

Breathe in. Breathe out.

What is something for which you are grateful?

Is it possible God did that?

How can you express gratitude and adoration to Him for that thing?

In your woundedness, can you still find the blessings? Where?

CHAPTER 7 / THE "AND IF NOT"

What is your "and if not"?

Do you believe that God is still worth trusting in the midst of your "and if not"?

How are you seeking Him?

CHAPTER 8 / AND YET

What are the truths that you believed about worship before your wounding?

What are the truths you believe about worship now?

In what is your understanding of worship grounded or secured?

CHAPTER 9 / PRACTICING

Where is beauty, even in the mess?

Where is hope, even in the despair?

Where is life, even in the pain?

Where is love, even in the mourning?

CHAPTER 10 / A NEW PERSPECTIVE

What do you hear that reminds you of God's love and His mercy?

What do you smell that reminds you of God's love and His mercy?

What do you see that reminds you of God's love and His mercy?

What do you taste that reminds you of God's love and His mercy?

What do you touch or feel that reminds you of God's love and His mercy?

CHAPTER 11 / I AM. I WILL.

Who are you?

What is true about you?

What makes you "you"?

What describes you?

What matters to you?

Who are you?

CHAPTER 12 / REMEMBER

Is there someone you fear forgetting?

Who was he/she?

What was true about him/her?

What made him/her "him/her"?

What described him/her?

What mattered to him/her?

Who was he/she?

CHAPTER 13 / THIS SIDE OF HEAVEN

What healing step have you been putting off doing since your wounding?

What small steps can you take toward that healing step?

Breathe in. What makes you feel gratitude?

Breathe out. What makes you feel adoration?

Remember: wounded is a part of you, but wounded is not all of you.

Acknowledgements

To my writing coach, the amazing Emily Osburne – I had no idea that my tentative direct message on social media would lead to the whirlwind of the past few months. Countless phone calls, texts, and emails, all filled with unending words of encouragement, advice, and wisdom… You have been absolutely irreplaceable on this book writing journey, my friend. Thank you for your help every step of the way.

To my editor, the brilliant Sarah Jo Land – I cannot begin to tell you how much I appreciate you being a part of this project with me. In the midst of your own busy life, you gave so generously of your time and your talent. Your insight has been absolutely priceless, my dear. Thank you for being so intentional and kind.

To my cover artist, the ever talented Dan Crosby - The moment I told Garry about my vision for the *And Yet* cover, we immediately thought of you. You listened to my ideas, asked really helpful questions, and created something absolutely beautiful. Thank you, thank you, thank you! I believe we owe you more than just a milkshake.

To my designer, Ms. Heather Dauphiny – This book would not be what it is without your creative eye. Thank you for listening to my vision and bringing it to life. Your unending patience with my endless thoughts, edits, and tweaks meant so much. I would not have been able to bring this to fruition without your help.

To my "first read" friends, my inner circle, and my cheerleaders – Where do I begin? Thank you for the encouraging texts. Thank you for the prayers. Thank you for the listening ears, the shoulders to cry on, the inappropriate jokes, the coffee, the wine, the hopeful voicemails, and so very much more. As scared as I have been to put these words out into the world for all to read, you have given me confidence. Your emotional, spiritual, financial, and even physical support have been more important to me than I can adequately put into words. Thank you for being with me and for me - both literally and figuratively. I am blessed beyond my merit.

To my Daddy, my big sister, and my baby brother – You did not have to trust me to tell our story. Though this book is from my perspective, it is our story. Thank you for trusting me. Thank you for encouraging me and believing in me. Though our family will never be the same without Sweet Momma, we are in it together. And for that, I am forever grateful. I love you – infinity...

To my three wonderful children – You have been such lights in the darkness, my dears. The fact that you call me "mom" is an absolute gift. Thank you for making me smile, helping me dance, crying with me, laughing with me, hoping with me and dreaming with me. I love you, infinity and beyond.

To my husband, the love of my life and my absolute favorite human being – What a gift it is to do life with you by my side. We have walked through so many moments and seasons together. Highs, lows, good, bad, beauty, devastation, joy, sorrow. You have been a constant source of joy, hope, wisdom, guidance, conviction, comfort, and light. Thank you for believing in me, inspiring me, and adventuring with me. I am grateful for the gift of you, my love. Always...

About the Author

ABBIE LYNN ABBOTT is many things – musician, dancer, writer, teacher, city girl, farm girl, Hoosier, Floridian, wife, daughter, sister, aunt, mother, friend. Of all of her accomplishments and titles though, Abbie is most proud of her family. Abbie and her husband, both born and raised in Indiana, now live in Florida with their three children. Abbie has written various blogs over the years (some of which can be found at www.thisabbottday.wordpress.com), but this is her first book. Her passions include caring for vulnerable children and families, experiencing and appreciating diversity and culture, and bringing hope and light to a world that desperately needs it.

For speaking engagements and other requests - Abbie can be reached at thisabbottday@gmail.com

Made in the USA
Monee, IL
14 May 2022